Designer Handbag Hustle: Thrifting and Reselling Luxury Accessories

By Silas Meadowlark

Index

- The Allure of Luxury Accessories
  - Understanding the Luxury Handbag Market
  - Recognizing Authentic Luxury Brands
  - Mastering the Art of Secondhand Shopping

- Thrifting for Treasure
  - Scouring Thrift Stores and Garage Sales
  - Identifying Hidden Gems
  - Tips for Negotiating Prices

- Online Sourcing Strategies
  - Navigating Online Marketplaces
  - Spotting Deals on Auction Sites
  - Building Relationships with Sellers

- Authenticating Luxury Handbags
  - Understanding Serial Numbers and Tags
  - Spotting Counterfeit Goods
  - Developing an Eye for Quality

- Cleaning and Refurbishing
  - Leather Conditioning and Restoration
  - Hardware Polishing and Repair
  - Fabric and Lining Rejuvenation

- Photographing and Listing
  - Capturing Captivating Images
  - Crafting Compelling Descriptions
  - Optimizing Listings for Visibility

- Pricing for Profit
  - Researching Market Trends
  - Calculating Cost of Goods Sold

- Setting Competitive Prices

- Shipping and Packaging
  - Selecting the Right Shipping Supplies
  - Ensuring Safe and Secure Delivery
  - Managing Returns and Exchanges

- Building Your Brand
  - Developing a Unique Seller Identity
  - Engaging with Online Communities
  - Leveraging Social Media Platforms

- Scaling Your Business
  - Streamlining Inventory Management
  - Outsourcing Tasks and Responsibilities
  - Navigating Legal and Tax Considerations

- Sourcing at Wholesale Events
  - Attending Trade Shows and Auctions
  - Negotiating Bulk Discounts
  - Diversifying Your Product Offerings

- Collaborating with Influencers
  - Identifying Relevant Influencers
  - Crafting Mutually Beneficial Partnerships
  - Leveraging Influencer Marketing

- Embracing Sustainability
  - Repurposing and Upcycling
  - Responsible Disposal of Damaged Items
  - Promoting Eco-Friendly Practices

- Navigating Regulations and Taxes
  - Understanding Sales Tax Requirements
  - Complying with Consumer Protection Laws
  - Maintaining Accurate Financial Records

- Adapting to Industry Changes
  - Staying Informed on Market Trends

- Anticipating Shifts in Consumer Preferences
- Diversifying Your Product Portfolio

The Allure of Luxury Accessories

Understanding the Luxury Handbag Market

The world of luxury accessories is a captivating realm where status, craftsmanship, and exclusivity collide. Luxury handbags, in particular, have long been the holy grail for fashion enthusiasts and style aficionados alike. These coveted items are more than just functional accessories – they are symbols of aspiration, symbols that whisper tales of refined taste and deep pockets. But examine deeper, and you'll find a dynamic, ever evolving scene that offers opportunities for the savvy and the bold.

To truly understand the luxury handbag market, one must first appreciate the intricacies that define it. These bags are not mere vessels for our belongings; they are meticulously crafted, often by hand, using the finest materials and techniques. From the supple Italian leathers to the gleaming hardware, every detail is carefully considered, infusing each piece with an unparalleled sense of luxury.

Brands like Chanel, Louis Vuitton, and Hermès have cultivated an aura of exclusivity that transcends mere materialism. Their names alone evoke images of elegant soirees, private jets, and the upper echelons of society. These are the hallmarks of a market that thrives on scarcity, on the idea that the most covetable items are those that are the most difficult to obtain.

But the true allure of luxury handbags lies in their ability to transform our everyday lives. A well chosen bag can improve a simple outfit, imbuing the wearer with a sense of confidence and sophistication. It becomes a reflection of our personal style, a sartorial statement that speaks volumes about our taste and aspirations.

Recognizing Authentic Luxury Brands

In the world of luxury accessories, authenticity is of great importance. As the demand for these coveted items grows, so too does the prevalence of counterfeit goods. Navigating the treacherous waters of luxury brand authentication can be a daunting task, but with the right knowledge and a distinguishing eye, you can learn to separate the genuine from the imitations.

The first step in recognizing authentic luxury brands is to familiarize yourself with the hallmarks of each label. From the iconic Chanel double c logo to the distinctive Hermès orange box, these visual cues are the calling cards of true luxury. But it goes beyond just the surface level details – delving deeper, you'll find that each brand has its own unique construction techniques, hardware finishes, and even the way the leather is treated and aged.

Serial numbers, date codes, and holographic tags are also important elements in the authentication process. These tiny, often hidden details can be the difference between a genuine Birkin and a clever forgery. Developing an eye for these nuances takes time and practice, but the rewards are immense – the confidence of knowing you've secured the real deal.

Of course, authenticity isn't just about the physical attributes of the bag; it's also about the intangible qualities that define a luxury brand. The stories behind each piece, the rich heritage, and the unwavering commitment to quality – these are the elements that truly boost a handbag from mere commodity to a cherished investment.

Mastering the Art of Secondhand Shopping

In the high stakes world of luxury accessories, the thrill of the hunt is unparalleled. While the allure of a brand new, freshly minted handbag is undeniable, the true treasure lies in the world of secondhand shopping. It's here, amid the racks and shelves of thrift stores, consignment shops, and online marketplaces, that the savvy shopper can uncover hidden gems – designer bags, often in pristine condition, at a fraction of their retail price.

The key to mastering the art of secondhand shopping is to develop a keen eye and an unwavering sense of patience. These prized possessions don't simply fall into your lap; they require persistence, dedication, and a willingness to sift through the proverbial haystack to find the needle. Whether it's combing through the racks at your local Goodwill or scrolling endlessly through online listings, the thrill of the hunt is what separates the casual shopper from the true luxury reseller.

But it's not just about finding the elusive designer bag; it's about understanding its value and negotiating a fair price. Research market trends, familiarize yourself with current resale values, and be prepared to engage in a delicate dance of offer and counter offer. The art of haggling is a skill to be honed, and the rewards can be substantial – the ability to secure a prized possession at a deep discount is the hallmark of a savvy secondhand shopper.

Lastly, remember that secondhand shopping is not just about the financial savings; it's about the thrill of the hunt and the satisfaction of uncovering a hidden gem. The rush of spotting a Chanel handbag nestled among the clutter, or the delight of negotiating a deal on a like new Louis Vuitton – these are the experiences that fuel the passion of the luxury reseller.

Thrifting for Treasure

Scouring Thrift Stores and Garage Sales

Attention all treasure hunters! The true allure of the luxury handbag hustle lies in the thrill of the hunt. While the big name retailers and online marketplaces may seem like the easy option, the real magic happens when you venture into the wild, untamed world of thrift stores and garage sales. It's here, amidst the racks of well worn clothing and the piles of dusty trinkets, that you'll uncover hidden gems just waiting to be polished and resold for a tidy profit.

Now, I know what you're thinking: "Thrift stores? Garage sales? Aren't those just full of junk?" Ah, my friend, that's where you're mistaken. The key is to approach these is a goldmine with the keen eye of a seasoned luxury hunter. Look past the stained t shirts and the mismatched socks, and focus your gaze on the unexpected – that designer handbag tucked away in the corner, the vintage Chanel brooch buried beneath a stack of books, the Hermès scarf hiding in plain sight. It's all about retraining your brain to see the potential where others see only discarded belongings.

But this thrifting game is not for the faint of heart. It requires a certain level of tenacity, a willingness to dig deep, and a healthy dose of good old fashioned luck. You'll need to navigate crowded aisles, sift through piles of clutter, and be prepared to act fast when you spot that elusive designer find. It's not for the faint of heart, but trust me, the payoff is worth it. Imagine the look on your customer's face when you present them with a beautifully refurbished Prada bag at a fraction of the retail price. Priceless, my friends, absolutely priceless.

Identifying Hidden Gems

Ah, the thrill of the hunt – it's like a game of high stakes hide and-seek, but with luxury handbags as the prize. As you scour those thrift store racks and garage sale tables, keep your eyes peeled for the unexpected. Look beyond the surface level flaws and focus on those subtle details that set a designer piece apart from the rest.

Start by familiarizing yourself with the hallmarks of luxury brands – the distinctive hardware, the carefully stitched logos, the unmistakable leather quality. Train your eye to spot the telltale signs of authenticity, because trust me, those counterfeiters are getting craftier by the day. Develop a keen sense of what to look for, whether it's the precise placement of a Gucci badge or the subtle embossing on a Louis Vuitton canvas.

But the real challenge lies in recognizing potential where others see only used and abused. That heavily worn Chanel tote? With a little love and elbow grease, it could be transformed into a showstopper. That Fendi clutch with a broken zipper? A quick repair and it'll be good as new. The key is to look past the surface level imperfections and see the true value beneath the grime and neglect.

Of course, this kind of discernment takes time and practice. Spend hours poring over authentication guides, consult with seasoned resellers, and trust your instincts. The more you immerse yourself in the world of luxury goods, the better you'll become at spotting those hidden gems that will set your business apart from the competition. Happy hunting, my fellow thrifting enthusiasts!

Tips for Negotiating Prices

Navigating the art of price negotiation is a delicate dance, my friends – one that requires equal parts charm, savvy, and a healthy dose of chutzpah. As you dive headfirst into the world of thrift store treasure hunting, you'll quickly learn that the sticker price is just the starting point. The real magic happens when you can deftly negotiate your way to a deal that leaves both you and the seller satisfied.

The key is to approach each interaction with a confident yet friendly demeanor. Remember, these sellers are individuals, not faceless corporations – appeal to their humanity and find common ground. Compliment their eye for hidden gems, commiserate over the challenges of running a small business, and above all, be respectful. A little bit of genuine rapport can go a long way in softening the bargaining process.

Of course, it's not all just sweet talk and warm fuzzies. You'll need to come armed with data – research the current market value of the item, be aware of recent sales trends, and know your numbers inside and out. This will give you the ammunition you need to make a persuasive case for your offer, one that demonstrates your expertise and your commitment to a fair deal.

And don't be afraid to get creative with your negotiating tactics. Perhaps you can offer to take the item off their hands immediately, saving them the hassle of having to store or display it. Or maybe you can sweeten the pot by promising to promote their business through your social media channels. The possibilities are endless, so long as you approach each interaction with a spirit of collaboration and mutual benefit.

Remember, the true art of thrifting lies in the negotiation. Embrace the challenge, sharpen your skills, and watch as those hard won discounts translate into tidy profits down the line. Happy haggling, my fellow luxury hustlers!

Online Sourcing Strategies

Navigating Online Marketplaces

In the fast paced world of luxury reselling, being able to navigate online marketplaces like a pro is important to your success. These digital hubs are teeming with hidden gems, but it takes a keen eye and a deft touch to uncover them. Forget the generic search bars - dive headfirst into the niche corners of these platforms, where the true is a goldmine lie. Nurture a sixth sense for the obscure and the overlooked, because that's where the real money is made.

Don't be afraid to get hands on and dig deep. Scour the listings, sifting through page after page of seemingly unremarkable items. Hone your instincts, training your eye to spot the potential in the seemingly mundane. That dull colored handbag? It could be a vintage Hermès waiting to be polished back to its former glory. The worn out leather tote? It might just be a coveted Chanel classic in need of a little TLC. Keep an open mind and a keen eye, and you'll be swimming in luxury loot before you know it.

Remember, the key to success in these online marketplaces is to think outside the box. Don't just search for the big name brands - branch out and explore the lesser known labels, the hidden gems that the masses have yet to discover. Be the first to uncover these untapped treasures, and you'll be sitting pretty with a trove of one of-a kind items that will have your customers clamoring for more.

Spotting Deals on Auction Sites

Auction sites can be a veritable minefield for the uninitiated, but with the right strategy, you can navigate these treacherous waters and emerge victorious, your arms laden with luxury spoils. The key is to approach these online auctions with the tenacity of a seasoned treasure hunter and the cunning of a seasoned negotiator.

First and foremost, do your homework. Scour the listings, research the brands, and familiarize yourself with the going rates. Arm yourself with knowledge, and use it to your advantage. When the bidding frenzy begins, stay cool, calm, and collected. Don't get caught up in the emotional rollercoaster of the auction – let your well honed instincts guide you. Know when to strike and when to hold back, and you'll walk away with the spoils of your victory.

But the real secret to success on these auction sites? Building relationships. Grow a network of trustworthy sellers, and establish yourself as a reliable, recognizing buyer. These connections can open doors to exclusive listings, off the-radar deals, and insider information that will give you a distinct edge over the competition. So take the time to nurture these relationships, and watch as the luxury bargains start rolling in.

Building Relationships with Sellers

In the high stakes world of luxury reselling, relationships are the lifeblood of your business. It's not just about finding the hidden gems – it's about building trust, promoting loyalty, and creating a network of reliable sellers that will keep you flush with the most coveted items.

Start by approaching every interaction with a genuine sense of respect and appreciation. These sellers are the gatekeepers to a goldmine of luxury goods, and you'll need to earn their trust before they'll share their best finds. Take the time to get to know them, to understand their needs and concerns, and to demonstrate your commitment to being a reliable and trustworthy partner.

But don't just be a passive observer – be proactive and creative in your approach. Offer value added services, like quick payments, hassle free returns, or even the occasional gift or gesture of appreciation. Show them that you're not just another faceless buyer, but a true collaborator who is invested in their success. And when you do land a killer deal, be sure to share the love – a little bit of reciprocity can go a long way in cementing those essential relationships.

Remember, in this game of luxury reselling, your network is your net worth. So nurture those connections, nurture those relationships, and watch as the doors to the most coveted luxury goods swing wide open, revealing a world of untold riches and limitless possibilities.

Authenticating Luxury Handbags

Understanding Serial Numbers and Tags

Ah, the complicated dance of authenticating luxury handbags – it's like solving a high stakes mystery where the clues are hidden in the most unexpected places. Let me let you in on a little secret: serial numbers and tags are the Sherlock Holmes of the luxury accessory world. These inconspicuous details can open up a abundance of information, separating the real deal from the cheap imitations faster than you can say "fake Fendi."

First up, serial numbers. These elusive strings of numbers and letters are the blueprints of a luxury handbag's identity. Each one is as unique as a fingerprint, meticulously etched into the leather or hardware by the brand's master craftsmen. But here's the catch: you can't just take the seller's word for it. No, my friend, you need to dive deep, uncover the nuances, and become a serial number sleuth extraordinaire.

And what about those pesky little tags, you ask? Oh, they're the MVP of the authentication game. From holographic labels to heat stamped logos, these tiny tokens of luxury hold the key to opening up a bag's provenance. But beware – counterfeiters are getting craftier by the day, so you'll need to develop an eagle eye for even the subtlest of discrepancies.

Now, I know what you're thinking: "But how do I become a master of serial numbers and tags?" Fear not, my distinguishing thrifter, for I've got your back. It's all about immersing yourself in the world of luxury brands, studying their signature elements, and honing your skills like a professional art appraiser. Trust me, once you've got the hang of it, you'll be spotting fakes from a mile away, leaving those counterfeiters trembling in their boots.

Spotting Counterfeit Goods

Let's talk about the elephant in the room: counterfeit goods. These crafty imitations are the bane of every savvy luxury reseller's existence, lurking around every corner, ready to trip up the unsuspecting. But fear not, my fellow treasure hunters, for with the right tools and a keen eye, you can become a counterfeit crushing ninja.

First and foremost, you need to develop a keen sense of detail – those pesky counterfeiters may think they've got it all figured out, but even the slightest imperfection can be your saving grace. From uneven stitching to misaligned hardware, these tiny tells can expose a fake faster than a magician revealing their trick.

But it's not just about the physical attributes, oh no. You need to become a master of the intangible as well. The weight, the smell, the overall quality – these are the subtle nuances that separate the real deal from the cheap knockoffs. It's like a secret language that only the true luxury connoisseurs can decipher.

And let's not forget about the importance of research. Staying up to-date on the latest authentication techniques, brand histories, and market trends is essential in your quest to become a counterfeit crushing extraordinaire. After all, knowledge is power, and in the world of luxury reselling, it's the difference between making a killing and getting killed.

Developing an Eye for Quality

Now, let's talk about the holy grail of luxury authentication: developing an eye for quality. It's not just about spotting the fakes – it's about being able to perceive the true masterpieces, the ones that will have your customers drooling with envy and your bank account bursting at the seams.

It all starts with a in-depth look into the world of luxury craftsmanship. Get to know the materials, the construction methods, the subtle nuances that separate the ordinary from the extraordinary. Familiarize yourself with the signature styles, the hallmarks of each prestigious brand, until you can spot a Chanel from a mile away, even in the most poorly lit thrift store.

But developing an eye for quality isn't just about head knowledge – it's about honing your senses, training your fingers to caress the supple leather and your eyes to scrutinize the perfect stitching. It's about becoming a luxury connoisseur, a true master of the craft, able to separate the diamond in-the rough from the cheap costume jewelry with a single glance.

And let me tell you, my friends, the rewards of this pursuit are bountiful. Imagine the thrill of scooping up a vintage Hermès bag for a song, only to turn around and sell it for a small fortune. Or the satisfaction of spotting a hidden gem amidst the chaos of a garage sale, knowing that you're about to make a killing. It's the stuff of reselling legends, and it's all yours for the taking – if you're willing to put in the work and develop that critical eye for quality.

Cleaning and Refurbishing

Leather Conditioning and Restoration

When it comes to luxury handbags, preserving the integrity of the leather is very important. After all, these bags are designed to be cherished for a lifetime, not tossed aside like a cheap knockoff. So, buckle up, because we're about to go on a journey of leather rejuvenation that would make even the snobbiest of fashion curators swoon.

First and foremost, let's talk conditioning. Think of it as a spa day for your bag - a little pampering can go a long way. Start by selecting a high quality leather conditioner that's specifically formulated for the type of leather you're working with. Trust me, you don't want to be that person who tries to use car wax on their Hermès. It's a recipe for disaster, and your bag will end up looking like a used tire.

Now, the application process is where the real magic happens. Gently massage the conditioner into the leather, working it in with small, circular motions. Pretend you're a world class masseuse, but instead of sore muscles, you're soothing the tired, weathered hide of your thrifted treasure. Once you've covered every inch, let the conditioner soak in for a bit, then buff the surface with a soft cloth to reveal a lustrous, hydrated finish.

But what if your bag is in dire need of some serious TLC? Fear not, my fellow thrifting aficionado, because restoration is an art form that we've perfected. Start by assessing the damage - is it a scuff, a scratch, or a full blown case of leather cracking and peeling? Depending on the severity, you may need to bring in the big guns, like leather dyes, sealants, and even professional repair services.

Remember, the key to successful restoration is patience and attention to detail. It's not just about slapping on a quick fix and calling it a day. No, this is a delicate dance, a symphony of leather coddling techniques that will have your bag looking brand new, or even better than the day it first graced the shelves of your favorite luxury retailer.

Hardware Polishing and Repair

Alright, let's talk about the unsung heroes of the luxury handbag world: the hardware. Those shiny, gleaming zippers, clasps, and rivets aren't just there for aesthetic appeal, they're the backbone that holds your prized possession together. And when they start to lose their luster, it's time to bust out the polish and get to work.

First and foremost, you'll want to assess the condition of the hardware. Is it simply dull and in need of a good shine, or is there more serious damage like corrosion or even missing pieces? Depending on the severity, you may need to enlist the help of a professional repair service, but don't worry, we'll walk you through the basics.

For a simple polish job, start by gently cleaning the hardware with a soft cloth and a mild, metal safe cleaner. Avoid anything too abrasive, as you don't want to risk scratching or damaging the delicate finishes. Once the surface is clean, apply a small amount of metal polish and buff it in with a soft, dry cloth. Keep buffing until you see that brilliant, showroom worthy shine.

But what if the hardware is in need of more serious attention? Maybe a clasp is broken, or a zipper is stuck? Well, my friend, that's where your inner MacGyver needs to come out and play. Start by carefully disassembling the troublesome component, taking note of how it all fits together. With a steady hand and the right tools, you can often repair or replace the damaged parts, bringing your bag back to its former glory.

Remember, when it comes to luxury hardware, patience and precision are key. Take your time, work carefully, and don't be afraid to seek out professional help if you're in over your head. After all, the last thing you want is to end up with a handbag that's more duct tape than designer.

Fabric and Lining Rejuvenation

Alright, let's talk about the forgotten stepchildren of the luxury handbag world: the fabric and lining. Sure, the leather and hardware may get all the attention, but these often overlooked elements are just as critical to the overall condition and value of your thrifted treasure.

First up, the fabric. Whether it's a delicate satin or a sturdy canvas, you're going to want to treat it with the same care and attention as the rest of the bag. Start by giving it a gentle once over with a clean, soft bristled brush, gently removing any accumulated dust or debris. Then, depending on the fabric type, you may need to employ a specialized cleaning solution or even a gentle spot cleaning method.

But don't stop there, my friend. Once the fabric is clean, it's time to work on restoring its vibrancy and luster. Break out the fabric protector spray and give the surface a light, even coating. This will help repel dirt and stains, keeping your bag looking fresh and fabulous for years to come.

Now, let's move on to the lining - the unsung hero that keeps the contents of your bag safe and secure. Over time, the lining can become discolored, frayed, or even develop unsightly stains. Fear not, because with a little elbow grease and some creative problem solving, you can make that lining look as good as new.

Start by gently cleaning the lining with a mild fabric cleaner, being careful not to soak the material. Once it's dry, you can try your hand at a little DIY lining restoration. Think about using a fabric marker to touch up any discoloration, or even sewing in a fresh patch of material to cover up stubborn stains. The possibilities are endless, and the end result will be a bag that looks like it just came off the showroom floor.

Remember, when it comes to luxury handbag rejuvenation, the devil is in the details. So, don't be afraid to get your hands a little dirty and release your inner fashion MacGyver. After all, with a little elbow grease and a whole lot of creativity, that thrifted gem can become the envy of every style savvy shopper in town.

Photographing and Listing

Capturing Captivating Images

Listen up, folks, because I'm about to let you in on a little secret: the key to selling those luxe handbags like hotcakes isn't just in the item itself, but in how you present it to the world. And when it comes to photography, let me tell you, you better bring your A game if you want to stand out in the digital jungle.

First and foremost, ditch the dingy garage lighting and the blurry smartphone snaps. You're selling high end goods, so you need to treat them like the stars they are. Invest in a decent DSLR camera, and learn to use it like a pro. Experiment with different angles, play with the depth of field, and for heaven's sake, make sure those shots are sharp and crystal clear.

But it's not just about the technical aspects, my friends. Nope, you've got to infuse a little bit of that je ne sais quoi into your images. Forget the boring, lifeless product shots - instead, think about telling a story. Stage your handbag in an elegant, aspirational setting, like a chic urban loft or a sun drenched seaside terrace. Accessorize it with some tasteful props, like a designer scarf or a sleek pair of sunglasses, to add a touch of sophistication.

And let's not forget the power of lighting. Harsh, unflattering fluorescents will do you no favors, but a soft, diffused glow can work wonders. Experiment with natural light, or invest in some simple studio lighting equipment to create those dreamy, high end vibes.

Remember, your photos are the first thing potential buyers will see, so you need to make sure they're nothing short of captivating. Channel your inner fashion photographer and get creative, because let me tell you, the competition is fierce out there.

Crafting Compelling Descriptions

Alright, now that you've got those drool worthy photos, it's time to put on your wordsmith hat and craft some descriptions that will have buyers clamoring to snatch up your luxury goods.

First and foremost, forget the dry, boring product specs - you want to transport your audience to a world of opulence and elegance. Start with a killer opening line that hooks them in, like "Imagine strutting down the streets of Milan with this timeless Prada tote on your arm," or "Raise your everyday style with this stunning Chanel clutch that oozes effortless sophistication."

But don't stop there, my friend. Dive deep into the details, painting a vivid picture of the item's craftsmanship, materials, and history. Wax poetic about the supple Italian leather, the gleaming hardware, the discreet yet iconic branding. Transport your audience to a realm where they can almost feel the luxurious texture and imagine the compliments they'll receive.

And let's not forget the all important condition report. Sure, you might be tempted to gloss over a few minor flaws, but trust me, honesty is the best policy. Acknowledge any wear and tear, but Frame it in a way that showcases your commitment to transparency and quality. "This vintage Gucci satchel has been lovingly cared for over the years, with only minor signs of use that only add to its timeless charm."

Remember, your goal is to craft a description that not only informs but also inspires. Weave in a touch of storytelling, a dash of aspirational imagery, and a healthy dose of authenticity, and you'll have buyers salivating to add that must have handbag to their collection.

Optimizing Listings for Visibility

Alright, you've got your captivating photos and your compelling descriptions - now it's time to make sure your luxury handbag listings are primed for maximum visibility. Because let's face it, with the sheer volume of secondhand goods out there, standing out in the digital crowd is no easy feat.

First and foremost, nail down your keywords. Think about the terms your target buyers are likely to search for, and sprinkle them liberally throughout your listings. But don't just stuff them in willy nilly - weave them seamlessly into your descriptions, titles, and tags. "Vintage Chanel Quilted Leather Shoulder Bag" is infinitely more eye catching than "Chanel Bag."

And speaking of titles, treat them like the superhero sidekicks of your listings. Concise, punchy, and packed with those all important keywords, your titles should be the first thing that grabs a potential buyer's attention. Avoid generic, forgettable titles and instead, opt for something that pops, like "Exquisite Prada Saffiano Leather Satchel - Gently Used Condition."

But your listing optimization journey doesn't end there, my friends. Oh no, you've also got to master the art of the photo carousel. Strategically arrange your snaps to showcase the item from every angle, highlighting any unique details or selling points. And don't be afraid to get a little creative - throw in a lifestyle shot or two to really drive home that aspirational vibe.

Last but not least, keep a close eye on your performance metrics. Pay attention to which listings are generating the most interest, and use those observations to refine your strategy. Experiment with different keyword combinations, tweak your photo arrangements, and keep iterating until you've got a winning formula that has those luxury handbag buyers flocking to your virtual storefront.

Pricing for Profit

Researching Market Trends

When it comes to pricing your luxury handbag finds, forget playing it safe. This is the big leagues, where a single digit can make or break your profit margins. So, roll up those sleeves, dial up your inner data crunching detective, and get ready to uncover the secrets of the luxury resale market.

Start by scoping out the competition. Stalk those online marketplaces like a fashion forward ninja, taking note of how similar items are priced. But don't just settle for a quick glance - dive deeper. Analyze the sale histories, average selling prices, and even the bidding wars. This intel will be your secret weapon when it's time to set those prices.

And let's not forget about the ever evolving world of trends. Stay on top of the latest must have brands, styles, and materials by immersing yourself in the world of luxury fashion blogs, influencers, and industry reports. Heck, start your own secret society of luxury handbag enthusiasts if you have to. Knowledge is power, and in this game, it can translate directly into dollar signs.

Don't be afraid to get a little unconventional in your research, either. Scour social media for observations into what's capturing the hearts and wallets of your target audience. Eavesdrop on conversations at high end shopping malls. Heck, befriend a few personal shoppers – they'll have the scoop on the latest trends before anyone else.

Calculating Cost of Goods Sold

Alright, time to get down to the nitty gritty. You've scored that vintage Chanel like a boss, but now it's time to figure out how much it's really worth. Cue the spreadsheets and calculators, my friend.

First, let's talk about your cost of goods sold (COGS). This includes the price you paid for the handbag, any restoration or cleaning costs, and any fees associated with acquiring it. Don't forget to factor in things like shipping, handling, and even the time you spent scouring thrift stores or negotiating with sellers.

Here's a pro tip: keep meticulous records of your expenses. Trust me, when tax season rolls around, you'll be thanking your past self for being such a diligent bookkeeper. Plus, it'll help you identify where you can potentially cut costs and boost your profit margins.

Now, the real magic happens when you start crunching the numbers. Compare your COGS to the current market prices for similar items. This will help you determine the sweet spot for your listing – high enough to make a tidy profit, but not so astronomical that it scares away potential buyers.

Remember, pricing is an art, not a science. Be willing to experiment, test different strategies, and fine tune your approach. The more data you collect, the better you'll get at striking that perfect balance between profitability and market demand.

Setting Competitive Prices

Alright, you've done your homework, analyzed the market, and calculated your COGS. Now it's time to put on your best poker face and set those prices. But don't just slap a number on it and call it a day – there's a little more nuance to this game.

First and foremost, always price your items with the buyer in mind. Sure, you want to make a killer profit, but you also need to ensure your listings are competitive and attractive. Scan the competition and price your items just a hair below the average. This will help you stand out and catch the eye of savvy shoppers.

But don't just stop there. Sprinkle in a little psychological magic, too. Pricing an item at $499 instead of $500 can make all the difference in the world. It's a subtle trick, but one that can pay off big time in the long run.

And let's not forget about the power of bundling. Offering a "complete set" or a "luxury package" can not only justify higher prices, but it can also give your customers a sense of added value. Just be sure to crunch the numbers and ensure your bundle prices are still competitive.

Finally, keep a close eye on your sales data and customer feedback. Use that information to fine tune your pricing strategies, experiment with different approaches, and stay ahead of the curve. In the ever evolving world of luxury resale, the only constant is change – so be ready to adapt and thrive.

Shipping and Packaging

Selecting the Right Shipping Supplies

Alright, let's talk shipping - the unsung hero of your luxury resale empire. Sure, your handbags might be worth more than the GDP of a small country, but if you can't get them to your customers in one piece, you might as well just toss them in the dumpster and call it a day. So, listen up, because I'm about to share some seriously clutch tips on selecting the right shipping supplies.

First and foremost, forget about those flimsy cardboard boxes you've been using. Those things are about as sturdy as a toddler trying to bench press a Buick. Instead, invest in some high quality, double walled boxes that can withstand the rigors of the shipping gauntlet. Trust me, your customers don't want their $3,000 Hermès Birkin showing up on their doorstep looking like it got run over by a monster truck.

And don't even think about skimping on the packing materials. We're talking bubble wrap, packing peanuts, and those air filled pouches that make a satisfying "pop" sound when you squeeze them. Pile that stuff on like a pyromaniac stocking up for the apocalypse. Your goal is to create a veritable fortress around your precious cargo, one that can survive a direct hit from a cruise missile.

Oh, and while we're on the subject, ditch the plain old shipping labels and go for something a little more... eye catching. Think custom printed boxes with your logo, or maybe even a few well placed holographic stickers. After all, you're not just selling a handbag - you're selling a luxurious experience. And trust me, your customers are going to be way more impressed by a package that looks like it was shipped directly from the set of "Ocean's Eleven" than some generic brown box.

Ensuring Safe and Secure Delivery

Alright, now that you've got the perfect shipping supplies lined up, it's time to focus on getting your precious cargo to its destination in one piece. And let me tell you, the world of luxury handbag shipping is like a high stakes game of chess, where one wrong move can cost you everything.

First and foremost, always, always, always opt for a reputable, insured shipping carrier. We're talking the big guns - FedEx, UPS, DHL, the whole nine yards. Sure, it might cost a little more, but trust me, it's worth it. These guys have the resources and the know how to make sure your handbags arrive safe and sound, no matter what Mother Nature or the guy with the forklift at the local warehouse has in store.

And when it comes to tracking, don't mess around. Sign up for all the shipping notifications, the real time updates, the whole shebang. That way, you can keep a close eye on your packages and jump into action the moment something goes sideways. Because let me tell you, there's nothing worse than a customer calling you up, wondering where their $10,000 Chanel is, while you're frantically searching the couch cushions for the tracking number.

Oh, and one more thing - insurance. Sure, it's an extra expense, but trust me, it's worth its weight in gold. Because the last thing you want is for one of your high end beauties to get lost or damaged in transit, only to have to shell out the full retail price to make it right. With insurance, you can rest easy knowing that if something goes wrong, you've got a safety net to catch you.

Managing Returns and Exchanges

Alright, let's talk about the dreaded R word: returns. Yeah, I know, it's not the most glamorous part of the business, but trust me, it's a necessary evil. And if you want to keep your luxury resale empire running like a well oiled machine, you better have a rock solid returns and exchanges policy in place.

First and foremost, make sure your customers know exactly what they're getting into. Spell out your policies in crystal clear language on your website, in your listings, and on every single piece of documentation that goes out the door. We're talking return windows, condition requirements, shipping instructions - the whole nine yards. That way, there's no room for confusion or misunderstandings down the line.

And when it comes to actually processing those returns, don't be a total Scrooge. Sure, you want to protect your bottom line, but you also need to keep your customers happy. So, offer a generous return window - maybe 30 days or even longer - and make the process as smooth and painless as possible. After all, nothing says "I value your business" like a hassle free return experience.

Oh, and one more thing - keep a close eye on those exchanged items. You never know when you might stumble upon a hidden gem that someone tried to slip past you. So, give each and every one a thorough inspection before putting it back up for sale. And who knows, you might even find a few "imperfections" that you can use to negotiate a killer deal on your next sourcing trip.

Building Your Brand

Developing a Unique Seller Identity

In the wild world of luxury reselling, you need to stand out like a peacock in a flock of pigeons. Forget about blending in with the masses - it's time to embrace your inner eccentric and let your unique seller identity shine. After all, the thrill of the hunt and the art of the deal is what sets you apart from the rest.

Start by asking yourself a simple question: what makes you, well, you? Are you the sassy vintage vixen, curating a collection of retro Chanel and Dior stunners? Or perhaps you're the sleek minimalist, spotlighting pristine Prada and Céline masterpieces? Whichever persona you choose, own it with unwavering confidence. Your buyers aren't just purchasing a handbag - they're buying into your unique brand story.

Develop a distinct visual aesthetic that reflects your personal style. Curate an Instagram feed that oozes sophistication and exclusivity, with carefully crafted product shots and behind the-scenes glimpses into your thrifting adventures. Invest in high quality packaging and branding materials that boost the unboxing experience for your customers. Remember, in the world of luxury reselling, the devil is in the details, and every touchpoint is an opportunity to cement your brand identity.

But don't stop there - weave your personality into every aspect of your business, from the witty captions you write to the cheeky customer service responses you craft. Be bold, be unapologetic, and above all, be memorable. After all, in a sea of cookie cutter luxury resellers, the one who stands out the most is the one who's most likely to make a sale.

Engaging with Online Communities

In the ever evolving world of luxury reselling, connecting with like minded individuals is key to building a loyal following and expanding your reach. Think of it as the digital version of mingling at a high end fashion soirée - it's all about networking, collaborating, and sharing the thrill of the hunt.

Start by immersing yourself in the online communities that cater to your niche. Join Facebook groups, Reddit threads, and Discord servers where luxury aficionados congregate to swap stories, share tips, and indulge in their passion for all things designer. Engage actively by offering your expertise, asking thought provoking questions, and participating in lively discussions. Remember, this is not a one way street - the more you give, the more you'll receive in the form of valuable understanding, connections, and potential collaborations.

Don't be afraid to step out of your comfort zone and reach out to fellow resellers, even those you might consider competitors. In the world of luxury reselling, there's often more than enough pie to go around, and forming strategic partnerships can open up new avenues for growth. Collaborate on joint projects, such as themed product collections or exclusive sales events, to tap into each other's audiences and create a buzz that appeals with your shared customer base.

Finally, position yourself as an industry expert by sharing your expertise and realizations. Start a blog or podcast where you dive deep into the intricacies of luxury reselling, from authenticating designer goods to navigating the ever changing market trends. Become a go to resource for aspiring resellers and established players alike, and watch as your reputation and influence continue to grow.

Leveraging Social Media Platforms

In the digital age, social media is the ultimate canvas for showcasing your luxury reselling prowess. It's where you can curate a visually stunning brand, forge meaningful connections with your audience, and position yourself as a trusted authority in the industry.

Start by identifying the social media platforms that match best with your target market. Is your audience primarily on Instagram, captivated by the allure of beautifully curated product shots and behind the-scenes glimpses? Or do they prefer the more conversational nature of Twitter, where you can engage in real time discussions and share your unfiltered thoughts? Tailor your content strategy to the unique strengths and preferences of each platform, and watch as your following grows exponentially.

When it comes to creating social media content, think beyond the standard product listings. Share the stories behind your latest thrifting finds, the art of negotiating with sellers, and the joy of restoring a vintage handbag to its former glory. Inject your personality into every post, whether it's a humorous anecdote or a thought provoking industry insight. Remember, your followers aren't just interested in the handbags - they're invested in your journey as a luxury reseller.

Apply the power of influencer marketing to increase your reach and credibility. Identify fashion forward trendsetters with a loyal following and collaborate on exclusive product features, giveaways, or even co designed collections. By tapping into their existing audience, you can instantly gain access to a pool of potential customers who are already primed and ready to embrace your unique brand.

Ultimately, social media is the ultimate playground for luxury resellers. Embrace the platform's dynamic nature, experiment with different content formats, and stay ahead of the curve by anticipating the ever evolving preferences of your audience. With a strategic, authentic approach, you'll be well on your way to building a thriving, recognizable brand that dominates the luxury reselling setting.

Scaling Your Business

Streamlining Inventory Management

Listen up, my fellow luxury reselling mavens, because I'm about to let you in on a little secret that'll have your inventory management game running smoother than a hot knife through butter. Forget the days of scribbling notes on the back of receipts and losing track of that limited edition Hermès scarf you snagged at a garage sale. It's time to get organized, people.

First things first, ditch the spreadsheets and embrace the power of inventory management software. These bad boys will have you tracking every single item like a seasoned FBI agent. Scan barcodes, assign SKUs, and watch your stock levels dance before your eyes. Heck, some of these systems even integrate with your online selling platforms, so you can wave goodbye to the dreaded "Item no longer available" mishaps.

But wait, there's more! Utilizing storage solutions like shelving units, clear bins, and labeled boxes will transform your workspace into a luxury reseller's dream. Imagine being able to locate that elusive Chanel clutch in the blink of an eye, instead of tearing through piles of bags like a rabid raccoon. Trust me, your sanity (and your bottom line) will thank you.

And let's not forget about those pesky expiration dates. Stay on top of your inventory by implementing a "first in, first out" system. That way, you can ensure those designer goodies are reaching their new owners before they start collecting dust. After all, you want your customers to be strutting around in style, not sporting a vintage look that's a little too vintage.

Outsourcing Tasks and Responsibilities

Alright, let's face it - you're not a superhero (although that banana suit you wear might beg to differ). At some point, you're going to need to call in the reinforcements if you want your luxury reselling empire to truly soar. And I'm not just talking about those trusty sidekicks you've recruited from your local thrift store. Nope, it's time to start outsourcing, my friends.

Now, I know what you're thinking: "Outsourcing? Isn't that for the big shots with deep pockets?" Well, let me tell you, even the scrappiest of luxury resellers can benefit from a little outside help. Start by identifying the tasks that are sucking up your precious time, whether it's meticulously cleaning and conditioning those leather goods or spending hours crafting the perfect product descriptions.

See if you can find reliable freelancers or virtual assistants to handle the mundane stuff, freeing you up to focus on the real money makers. Trust me, it's a game changer. Imagine having someone else handle your shipping and packaging, leaving you to work on scouring the thrift stores for your next big score. Or how about outsourcing your photography to a savvy shutterbug who can make your items shine like the diamonds they are?

The key is to find the right balance – don't go overboard and outsource everything, but don't be afraid to delegate either. After all, you're the visionary, the trendsetter, the one who's going to take this luxury reselling game to new heights. So let the experts handle the heavy lifting while you do what you do best: hunt down those hidden gems and turn them into a serious cash cow.

Navigating Legal and Tax Considerations

Alright, let's talk about the not so-glamorous side of scaling your luxury reselling business: the legal and tax stuff. I know, I know, it's enough to make your eyes glaze over faster than a Krispy Kreme donut, but trust me, ignoring these important details can come back to haunt you faster than a '90s fashion trend.

First things first, make sure you've got your business structure sorted out. Are you flying solo as a sole proprietor, or have you taken the plunge and formed a limited liability company (LLC)? Believe me, the latter option can save you a world of headaches when it comes to liability and tax implications. Plus, it just sounds way more professional when you introduce yourself as "the CEO of Luxury Resale Extraordinaire, LLC."

And speaking of taxes, don't even think about trying to eyeball that stuff. Find yourself a savvy accountant who can help you navigate the murky waters of sales tax, income tax, and all the other financial regulations you need to keep on top of. Sure, it's an added expense, but trust me, it's a heck of a lot better than getting audited and having the IRS come knocking at your door.

Oh, and don't forget about those pesky shipping rules and regulations. Make sure you're up to date on the latest dos and don'ts when it comes to sending your precious cargo across state (or even international) lines. The last thing you want is to have your beloved Chanel boomerang back to you because you didn't properly declare the contents or slap on the right labels.

Look, I know all this legal and tax stuff can be a real buzz kill, but trust me, it's the difference between building a thriving, sustainable luxury reselling business and ending up in a world of trouble. So suck it up, get those spreadsheets and contracts in order, and keep your eye on the prize – those sweet, sweet profits that'll have you living the high life in no time.

Sourcing at Wholesale Events

Attending Trade Shows and Auctions

Dive into the high octane world of luxury handbag sourcing by attending trade shows and auctions. These bustling events are the breeding grounds for savvy resellers like yourself, where you'll find a dizzying array of designer goods at prices that'll make your heart race faster than a cheetah on red bull. But don't be fooled, my friend - navigating these crowds is an art form that requires finesse, cunning, and the reflexes of a ninja.

First things first, do your homework. Research the major trade shows and auction houses that specialize in luxury accessories. These are the places where you'll find the real gems, the unicorns that'll have your customers scrambling to empty their wallets. The key is to get in early, scope out the scene, and be ready to pounce like a hungry lion on its prey. Trust me, the early bird doesn't just get the worm - it gets the Hermès Birkin at a fraction of the retail price.

Now, when you're on the ground, it's time to release your inner detective. Scrutinize every bag, every buckle, every minuscule detail. Hone your eagle eye skills until you can spot a counterfeit from a mile away. And don't be afraid to get a little scrappy - a little friendly negotiation can go a long way in scoring the deal of a lifetime. Just remember, these sellers are seasoned pros, so bring your A game and be prepared to dazzle them with your knowledge and charm.

But the real magic happens when you start to network. Strike up conversations with other resellers, share tips and tricks, and build those critical connections. You never know when that random chat with the guy in the corner may lead to a game changing sourcing opportunity. It's all about cultivating those relationships, my friend, because in this cutthroat world of luxury handbag reselling, it's not just about what you know - it's about who you know.

Negotiating Bulk Discounts

Alright, let's talk about the art of the deal. You've scoured the trade shows, you've honed your authenticating skills, and now it's time to put on your best poker face and negotiate those bulk discounts. This is where the true hustle comes into play, my friend, so get ready to channel your inner Gordon Gekko.

First and foremost, come prepared. Research the current market prices, know your costs, and have a clear idea of your desired profit margins. Armed with this knowledge, you'll be able to negotiate like a seasoned pro, leaving those sellers sweating and wondering how you managed to pull off such a sweet deal.

But it's not just about the numbers, oh no. It's about building rapport, cultivating relationships, and making those sellers feel like they're getting just as much out of the deal as you are. Compliment their merchandise, share your expertise, and let them know that you're not just another reseller - you're a partner in their success. Trust me, a little charm can go a long way in securing those bulk discounts.

And remember, patience is key. Don't be afraid to walk away from a deal that doesn't feel quite right. The luxury handbag market is constantly in flux, and you never know when that elusive grail piece will come your way. Stay focused, stay disciplined, and never settle for anything less than the perfect opportunity.

So, embrace your inner negotiator, channel your inner Vin Diesel, and let the bargaining begin. Because when it comes to sourcing luxury accessories at wholesale events, the hustle is real, and the rewards are oh so-sweet.

Diversifying Your Product Services

In the high stakes world of luxury handbag reselling, it's all about keeping one step ahead of the competition. And that, my friends, means diversifying your product selections like a boss. Sure, you might be the Queen of Chanel, the Duchess of Dior, but don't let that lull you into a false sense of security. The market is constantly evolving, and you need to be ready to adapt, adjust, and expand your horizons like a support.

So, what does this mean in practical terms? It's time to start thinking outside the box, my friend. Don't just stick to the tried and true handbag brands - start exploring the world of luxury accessories. Think scarves, sunglasses, jewelry, even high end luggage. These items can not only diversify your inventory, but they can also open up a whole new world of sourcing opportunities.

And let's not forget about the power of collaboration. Forge partnerships with other resellers, pool your resources, and start sourcing at wholesale events as a team. Not only will this give you access to a wider range of products, but it'll also allow you to employ your collective buying power to score some truly jaw dropping deals.

But the real magic happens when you start to get creative. Embrace your inner artist and start exploring the world of customization and upcycling. Transform those well loved vintage pieces into one of-a kind works of art, and watch your customers go wild for your unique services. Who knows, you might just stumble upon the next big thing in the luxury accessories world.

So, get out there, take some risks, and embrace the thrill of the unknown. Because in this game, the true advocates for are the ones who are willing to think outside the box, push the boundaries, and constantly reinvent themselves. Are you ready to take your luxury handbag hustle to the next level?

Collaborating with Influencers

Identifying Relevant Influencers

The influencer marketing scene is a veritable minefield, fraught with Instagram models hawking detox teas and YouTube stars shilling dubious get rich-quick schemes. But fear not, my fellow luxury resellers - with a keen eye and a willingness to dive down the rabbit hole of social media, you can uncover a goldmine of influencers who will raise your brand to dizzying heights.

Start by casting a wide net. Scour the depths of your niche, searching for accounts that exude the perfect blend of style, authority, and engaged followership. Don't just look at the big names - sometimes, the most powerful partnerships can be forged with micro influencers whose audiences are laser focused and fiercely loyal.

Once you've identified a few promising candidates, it's time to put on your Sherlock Holmes hat. Dive into their content, analyze their engagement metrics, and get a feel for their aesthetic and personality. Are they a perfect fit for your luxury resale vibe, or would a collaboration feel like an awkward prom date?

Remember, compatibility is key. The most successful influencer partnerships are built on a foundation of shared values, mutual respect, and a genuine passion for the products or services being promoted. Tread carefully, and trust your gut - the wrong influencer can quickly turn your designer hustle into a designer disaster.

Crafting Mutually Beneficial Partnerships

Ah, the art of the influencer deal. It's a delicate dance, where the steps must be choreographed with precision to ensure that both parties waltz away feeling like winners. Because let's be real, no self respecting influencer is going to slap your brand all over their feed unless they're getting something juicy in return.

Start by offering more than just a fistful of cash. Think outside the box - free products, exclusive access, behind the-scenes content, or even a chance to co create something special. The key is to tap into their passions and provide genuine value, not just a paycheck.

But don't forget to protect your own interests, too. Negotiate terms that give you creative control, set clear performance expectations, and include provisions for terminating the partnership if things go south. After all, you're not just handing over the keys to your brand - you're entrusting it to someone whose own interests may not always harmonize with yours.

And remember, the true measure of a successful influencer collaboration isn't just the number of likes or sales. It's the way it seamlessly integrates your luxury resale brand into the influencer's authentic content, elevating both your profiles in the eyes of your target audience. Nail that, and you'll be well on your way to influencer fueled domination.

Leveraging Influencer Marketing

Once you've secured your dream influencer partnership, it's time to let loose the power of their platform and reach. But don't just hand over the reins and hope for the best - this is where the real magic happens, and you need to be an active participant.

Start by collaborating closely with your influencer to develop a content strategy that harmonizes with your brand's tone and messaging. Get creative - think beyond the standard product placement posts and tap into the influencer's unique storytelling abilities. Maybe they could showcase your latest designer score in an awe inspiring styling video, or give their followers a behind the-scenes look at your thrifting adventures.

And don't forget the power of social proof. Use your influencer's endorsement to drive traffic, boost engagement, and nurture a loyal community of luxury loving followers. Encourage them to share user generated content, engage with comments, and even offer exclusive discounts or giveaways to further strengthen the connection between your brand and their audience.

But the real secret to influencer marketing success? Staying flexible and adapting to the ever changing social media terrain. Keep a close eye on your metrics, be willing to shift your strategy, and never be afraid to try something new. Because in the world of luxury resale, the only constant is change - and the influencers who thrive are the ones who are always one step ahead of the curve.

Embracing Sustainability

Repurposing and Upcycling

Think outside the box, my friends. Just because that designer handbag has seen better days doesn't mean it's destined for the landfill. Nah, my fellow hustlers, we're about to free our inner MacGyver and transform those forgotten treasures into something truly spectacular.

Let's start with a little inspiration, shall we? Imagine taking that worn out Gucci tote and turning it into a chic laptop sleeve. Or how about that tired looking Chanel clutch becoming the centerpiece of a one of-a kind throw pillow? The possibilities are as endless as your creativity. Heck, I once saw a woman turn a Louis Vuitton scarf into a show stopping headband – and let me tell you, that thing flew off the shelves faster than a Kardashian at a sample sale.

The key is to approach each "damaged" item with a fresh perspective. Don't see flaws, see potential. That ripped lining? It's begging to be a funky patch on a denim jacket. That missing hardware? Time to get crafty with some metallic paint and a little elbow grease. Remember, one person's trash is another person's upcycled masterpiece.

Now, I know what you're thinking: "But Samantha, won't I be reducing the value of these luxury goods?" To which I say, pish posh! The true value lies in the creativity and sustainability you're bringing to the table. Think of it as taking a classic luxury item and giving it a whole new lease on life. Trust me, your customers will eat it up – they'll be lining up to snag your one of-a kind, eco chic creations.

Responsible Disposal of Damaged Items

Now, let's talk about the not so-glamorous side of this hustle: dealing with items that are truly beyond repair. It's a hard truth to face, but sometimes, even our most beloved luxury goods can reach the end of their lifespan. But fear not, my fellow thrifters – there are responsible ways to ensure these items don't end up polluting our planet.

First and foremost, always explore donation options. Reach out to local charities, shelters, or even luxury brand recycling programs to see if they can give that tired tote a new lease on life. You'd be surprised how many organizations are eager to repurpose or recycle these high quality materials.

But what if donation just isn't an option? Well, that's where the magic of proper disposal comes in. I'm talking about finding eco friendly ways to break down those materials and give them new life. Think about salvaging the hardware – those shiny buckles and zippers can be cleaned up and used for all sorts of crafty projects. As for the leather, fabric, and other components, research local recycling centers that specialize in textiles and materials.

And let's not forget about the packaging – those fancy dust bags and boxes are too good to just toss in the trash. Get creative and find ways to reuse or recycle them. Turn them into storage solutions, gift wrap, or even unique display pieces for your online shop. The key is to always be on the lookout for ways to minimize waste and maximize sustainability.

Promoting Eco Friendly Practices

As a savvy luxury goods reseller, it's not enough to simply embrace sustainability behind the scenes. Nope, we're going to shout our eco friendly practices from the rooftops – or at least, from the carefully curated corners of the internet.

Start by showcasing your sustainable efforts in your online listings. Highlight how you've repurposed or upcycled certain items, and let your customers know about the donation and recycling programs you support. Trust me, those eco conscious consumers will be drawn to your shop like moths to a very stylish flame.

But don't stop there – take it a step further by partnering with like minded brands and influencers. Collaborate on sustainability focused content, host thrifting workshops, or even organize beach cleanups. Not only will this help spread the word about your commitment to the planet, but it'll also forge valuable connections with a community that truly cares.

And let's not forget about the power of storytelling. Weave the narrative of your sustainable hustle into your brand identity. Share the inspiring tales of how you transformed a forgotten designer find into a one of-a kind masterpiece. Or highlight the charities and recycling programs you work with, and the tangible impact your efforts are making. When your customers see the heart and soul behind your business, they'll be even more invested in supporting your eco friendly mission.

Remember, being a responsible luxury reseller isn't just good for the planet – it's also a surefire way to differentiate yourself in a crowded market. So embrace those sustainable practices, shout them from the rooftops, and watch your business soar to new, eco chic heights.

Navigating Regulations and Taxes

Understanding Sales Tax Requirements

Ah, the joys of running a reselling business - where navigating the murky waters of sales tax can feel like tip toeing through a minefield blindfolded. But fear not, my fellow thrifting trailblazers, for we shall conquer this bureaucratic beast together!

First and foremost, it's critical to understand that sales tax requirements can vary wildly depending on your location. What might be a non issue in one state could land you in hot water in another. The key is to become an absolute sales tax detective, digging deep into the rules and regulations of every jurisdiction you operate in.

Start by familiarizing yourself with the sales tax policies in your home state. Research the thresholds for collection and remittance, the specific product categories that are taxable, and any unique exemptions or holidays that may apply. But don't stop there! Expand your investigative prowess to any other states where you sell, whether it's through online marketplaces or in person events.

And don't be fooled - just because you're dealing in secondhand goods, it doesn't mean you're automatically exempt from sales tax. In fact, many states view thrifted luxury items as fair game. So be prepared to collect and remit those taxes, lest you find yourself in the crosshairs of the tax authorities.

Remember, staying on top of your sales tax obligations is not only a legal requirement, but it can also be a strategic advantage. Properly accounting for taxes can help you price your items competitively and avoid any nasty surprises down the line. Embrace your inner tax nerd, my friends, and let's make sure the tax man is never knocking at your door!

Complying with Consumer Protection Laws

Ah, the joys of navigating the labyrinth of consumer protection laws - where one misstep can lead to a legal nightmare that makes even the bravest of resellers quiver in their thrifted boots. But fear not, my fellow luxury aficionados, for we shall conquer this legal scene with the grace and finesse of a seasoned diplomat.

First and foremost, it's essential to familiarize yourself with the consumer protection laws in your area. From truth in-advertising requirements to stringent rules around product descriptions, it's essential to stay on the right side of the law. After all, the last thing you want is to find yourself in a courtroom, defending your claims about that "gently used" Birkin bag.

But compliance goes beyond just the legal technicalities. It's also about cultivating a culture of trust and transparency within your business. Be upfront with your customers about the condition of your items, any known flaws or defects, and the steps you've taken to authenticate the luxury goods you're offering.

And speaking of authenticity, that's a whole other minefield to navigate. With the proliferation of counterfeit goods in the resale market, it's vital to have a rock solid authentication process in place. Familiarize yourself with the telltale signs of a fake, and never hesitate to err on the side of caution. After all, it's better to pass on a potential sale than to risk the wrath of an unhappy customer and the watchful eye of consumer protection agencies.

Remember, compliance with consumer protection laws is not just a box to check - it's a proof to the integrity of your business. By embracing a culture of transparency and authenticity, you'll not only stay out of legal trouble, but you'll also build a loyal customer base that trusts you to deliver high quality, genuine luxury goods. So let's don our legal capes and soar to new heights of reselling success!

Maintaining Accurate Financial Records

Ah, the joys of running a reselling business - where the thrill of the hunt for that elusive Chanel is matched only by the excitement of diving headfirst into a sea of spreadsheets and receipts. But fear not, my fellow luxury hustlers, for with the right approach, maintaining accurate financial records can be the key to uncovering the true potential of your reselling empire.

First and foremost, it's essential to establish a rock solid system for tracking your expenses. From the cost of those thrifted gems to the shipping supplies and professional services you employ, every penny must be accounted for. Trust me, when tax season rolls around, you'll be thanking your meticulous past self for keeping such a tight ship.

But it's not just about the expenses, my friends. Nay, the true power lies in meticulously documenting your sales as well. Maintain a detailed inventory of every item you've sold, complete with the purchase price, sales price, and any relevant profit margins. This information will not only help you identify your most lucrative product categories, but it will also serve as a essential resource when it comes to calculating your tax obligations.

And speaking of taxes, let's not forget the importance of keeping impeccable records for your tax filings. From tracking your sales tax remittances to compiling your income and expenses, every bit of data must be pristine and ready for the scrutiny of the tax authorities. After all, the last thing you want is to find yourself in a tangled web of audits and penalties, all because you couldn't keep your spreadsheets in order.

Remember, my fellow resellers, accurate financial records are the foundation upon which your luxury hustle will thrive. So embrace your inner accountant, grab those highlighters, and let's make sure your books are so clean, they could land you a gig as the personal financial advisor to the Kardashians. The path to reselling riches awaits!

Adapting to Industry Changes

Staying Informed on Market Trends

In the ever evolving world of luxury handbag reselling, staying on top of the latest market trends is essential for your success. It's not enough to simply source and sell - you need to be a savvy, well informed entrepreneur, constantly anticipating the next big shift in consumer preferences and industry dynamics.

Start by immersing yourself in the online communities where passionate luxury handbag enthusiasts congregate. Join forums, follow influential bloggers and vloggers, and engage with fellow resellers. These are the pulse points where you'll catch wind of emerging trends, new brand launches, and insider intel long before it hits the mainstream.

But don't just rely on digital sources. Get out there and mingle with the people who shape the industry. Attend luxury fashion events, pop up shops, and industry trade shows. Network with boutique owners, brand representatives, and fellow resellers. The connections you make and the conversations you have can provide essential understanding that give you a competitive edge.

Complement your networking efforts with in depth market research. Analyze sales data, track pricing fluctuations, and monitor the performance of various luxury brands and product categories. Employ tools like Google Trends, industry reports, and specialized market research platforms to uncover the nuances and shifting tides of the luxury handbag scene.

Remember, the more informed you are, the better equipped you'll be to navigate the ever changing terrain of the luxury resale market. Stay curious, stay connected, and stay one step ahead of the curve.

Anticipating Shifts in Consumer Preferences

In the fast paced world of luxury accessories, consumer preferences can shift as quickly as the seasons. What was once a coveted, must have item can quickly become passé, while new trends can emerge seemingly overnight. As a savvy reseller, your ability to anticipate and adapt to these changes will be the key to your long term success.

Keep a close eye on the aspirational influencers, tastemakers, and style icons who shape the desires of your target audience. Observe how their personal style and endorsements evolve, as this can provide valuable clues about the latest luxury handbag obsessions. Pay attention to the styles, brands, and features that are generating the most buzz on social media and fashion blogs.

But don't just rely on the opinions of the jet set elite. Engage directly with your customer base, whether through social media, email surveys, or in person interactions. Understand their is a challenge, their shopping habits, and their evolving needs. This hands on, customer centric approach will help you stay ahead of the curve and anticipate the next big shift in consumer preferences.

Be prepared to shift quickly when the market demands it. Invest time and resources into researching new luxury brands, exploring emerging product categories, and diversifying your inventory to ensure you're always offering the latest and greatest. Embrace the thrill of the hunt and the challenge of staying ahead of the curve - it's what separates the true luxury resale mavens from the also rans.

Diversifying Your Product Services

In the dynamic world of luxury resale, diversification is key to long term success. Relying solely on a single product category or brand can leave you vulnerable to market fluctuations and shifting consumer trends. By diversifying your product selections, you'll not only mitigate risk but also tap into new revenue streams and expand your customer base.

Start by exploring adjacent product categories within the luxury accessories sphere. Perhaps you've been focusing solely on handbags, but there's a wealth of opportunity in scarves, wallets, sunglasses, and even luxury jewelry. Diversifying your inventory allows you to cater to a wider range of customer preferences and improve your status as a one stop shop for perceiving luxury enthusiasts.

But don't stop there. Consider branching out into complementary product categories that harmonize with your customers' lifestyles and aspirations. Think high end home decor, gourmet food and beverage items, or even luxury tech accessories. By offering a curated selection of lifestyle products, you'll create a more immersive and engaging shopping experience that keeps your customers coming back.

Don't be afraid to experiment and take calculated risks. Stay adaptable and responsive to market demands, and be willing to adjust your product mix accordingly. Continuously research emerging trends, assess your sales data, and solicit feedback from your customer base to guide your diversification efforts. The more diverse and well rounded your inventory, the better positioned you'll be to weather any storm and capitalize on the ever changing tides of the luxury resale industry.

Silas Meadowlark

Printed in Great Britain
by Amazon